Zoom In on
Our Renewable Earth

Recycling

Andrea Rivera

abdopublishing.com

Published by Abdo Zoom™, PO Box 398166, Minneapolis, Minnesota 55439. Copyright © 2017 by Abdo Consulting Group, Inc. International copyrights reserved in all countries. No part of this book may be reproduced in any form without written permission from the publisher. Abdo Zoom™ is a trademark and logo of Abdo Consulting Group, Inc.

Printed in the United States of America, North Mankato, Minnesota
102016
012017

THIS BOOK CONTAINS
RECYCLED MATERIALS

Cover Photo: Shutterstock Images
Interior Photos: Shutterstock Images, 1, 6, 7, 9, 15, 19; Wave Break Media/Shutterstock Images, 4–5; Evan Lorne/Shutterstock Images, 8; Elena Elisseeva/Shutterstock Images, 10–11; iStockphoto, 13, 21; Brent Lewin/Bloomberg/Getty Images, 14; Ben Birchall/PA Wire URN:23574214/Press Association/AP Images, 17; Srisakorn Wonglakorn/Shutterstock Images, 18–19

Editor: Emily Temple
Series Designer: Madeline Berger
Art Direction: Dorothy Toth

Publisher's Cataloging-in-Publication Data
Names: Rivera, Andrea, author.
Title: Recycling / by Andrea Rivera.
Description: Minneapolis, MN : Abdo Zoom, 2017. | Series: Our renewable Earth |
    Includes bibliographical references and index.
Identifiers: LCCN 2016948926 | ISBN 9781680799408 (lib. bdg.) |
    ISBN 9781624025266 (ebook) | ISBN 9781624025822 (Read-to-me ebook)
Subjects: LCSH: Refuse and refuse disposal--Juvenile literature. | Recycling
    (Waste)--Juvenile literature. | Renewable energy sources--Juvenile literature
Classification: DDC 363.72/82--dc23
LC record available at http://lccn.loc.gov/2016948926

Table of Contents

Recycling is using materials more than once. It turns waste into something new. This **reduces** waste. It keeps the earth healthy, too.

Plastic and glass
are recycled.
So is paper.

One pound (0.5 kg) of recycled newspaper can make 2,000 sheets of writing paper.

Food waste can be recycled.
It is turned into **compost**.

Tiny **organisms** break down the waste.

Some people use compost in gardens. Compost gives soil **nutrients**. This helps plants grow.

Engineering

Machines help recycle plastic. They break the plastic into pieces. Ovens melt the plastic. It gets soft.

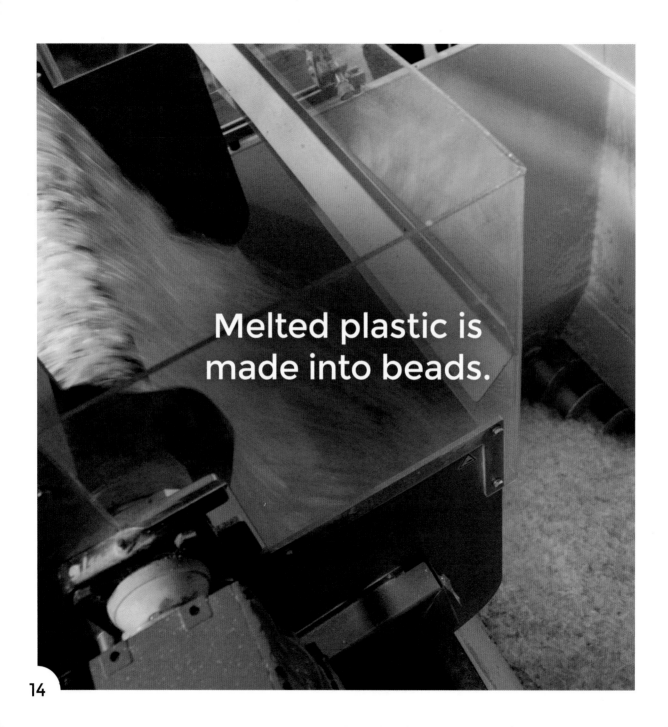

Melted plastic is made into beads.

The beads are used to make new plastic **products**.

Art

People can make art from trash.
Some artists recycled wood.
They made it look like whales.

They also made plastic bottles look like water.

Math

Americans use 2.5 million plastic bottles each hour. One day has 24 hours. About 60 million plastic bottles are used in one day.

But only about 18 million of those bottles are recycled.

- Recycling 1 ton (907 kg) of paper saves 17 trees.

- Many cans are made of aluminum. There is a lot of aluminum on Earth's surface. It can be recycled many times.

- Recycling one aluminum can saves enough energy to run a TV for three hours.

- Americans throw out enough glass bottles in one month to fill up a skyscraper.

Glossary

compost - a mixture of leaves, food waste, or other items that come from living things. Compost helps plants grow.

nutrient - a thing that plants and animals need to live and grow.

organism - a living animal or plant.

product - something that is made to be sold or used.

reduces - makes something smaller or less.

Booklinks

For more information
on recycling, please visit
booklinks.abdopublishing.com

Learn even more with the Abdo Zoom
STEAM database. Check out
abdozoom.com for more information.

Index